FINCHALE PR

COUNTY DURHAM

Peter Ryder

Finchale Priory owes its origin to Saint Godric, a colourful and heroic figure born about 1065 who, after years of travel as sailor, merchant and pilgrim, felt a call to the solitary life. He eventually settled at Finchale, where he lived to the remarkable age of 105.

In 1196, Godric's hermitage became a priory. After the troubled years of the mid-fourteenth century, the Finchale community was reduced in size, and took on a new role as a 'holiday place' for monks from the parent monastery at Durham. The priory church was reduced in size, and alterations and extensions made to the prior's house, which seems to have become the new focus of community life. The priory was dissolved in 1538, and the buildings gradually fell into ruin, until antiquarian interest grew in the nineteenth century and repair and conservation of the extensive remains were undertaken.

The story of Finchale can be read in its surviving remains, from St Godric's original church and tomb, through the thirteenth-century priory, to the remodelled buildings of the later medieval period.

❖ CONTENTS ❖

Published by English Heritage
1 Waterhouse Square, 138-142 Holborn, London EC1N 2ST
© English Heritage 2000
First published by English Heritage 2000.
Reprinted 2010.
Photographs, unless otherwise specified, were taken by English Heritage Photographic Unit and remain the copyright of English Heritage

Edited by Lorimer Poultney
Designed by Derek Lee
Plan by Ray Martin, Art Services Ltd
Printed in England by the colourhouse ltd, London
C10 06/10 08059   ISBN 978 1 85074 758 1

Mixed Sources
Product group from well-managed forests and other controlled sources
www.fsc.org Cert no. SGS-COC-2524
© 1996 Forest Stewardship Council
FSC

DESCRIPTION AND TOUR

THE CHURCH

A medieval visitor would have approached the priory church through its western doorway, and this is probably the best place to begin a tour of the ruins. So, from the entrance to the site, either go through the church, or round the end of the north transept, to stand outside the west end.

In front of you is the early thirteenth-century west front of the church, and on the right the tall gable of the monastic west range. The richly moulded west doorway (now much weathered) and three headless long narrow, or lancet, windows above are all of early thirteenth-century date. Behind you would have been the outer court with its barns, farm and administrative buildings (see 'The Precinct'). Only the church and central complex of monastic buildings lie within the railed guardianship area; the walled area or 'precinct' of the medieval priory covered a much larger area.

Looking through the west doorway towards the east end of the church

Nave
Go through the doorway into the nave.

Just inside the door is a surviving area of paved flooring, the slabs including two carved with simple crosses, probably grave stones. On either side of the nave area there are four arcades of thirteenth-century

Engraving for Thomas Dugdale's Monasticon, *1665, showing the priory before the collapse of the spire*

arches, with alternating round and octagonal pillars, blocked up with masonry. These arcades were blocked up in about 1364, when the traceried windows on the north were inserted. The south wall has no windows, and has been partially demolished, the arcade piers (two now reduced to their bases) being taken to be re-used in a horse-engine house on the nearby farm.

Walk east to the crossing in the centre of the church.

There must have been an altar here, as there are a piscina and aumbry (for washing and storing the vessels used in communion) set high up in the south wall, implying there was some sort of raised platform. The four massive circular piers supported a central tower with a spire. A drawing of 1665 shows it still complete, although it had fallen by the early eighteenth century. The north-west pier is hollow and contains a spiral stair.

South transept

The transepts contained several altars. In the south transept, beneath a large window of c.1300 in the east wall, is the base of what is thought to have been the altar of St Mary; on one side is an arched piscina and on the other an aumbry or wall cupboard, partly blocked by the base of a stone stair that once rose across the south gable of the transept to give access to a doorway into the monk's dormitory. This was the night stair, used by the monks during their nocturnal services. Later, when the original day stair was abandoned, a new opening was cut through the west wall of the transept to give direct access from the cloister for daytime use.

The site of the night stair to the monks' dormitory

North transept

The southern part of the north transept was built first in good-quality squared stonework; some foundations of what may have been its temporary north wall remain, before it was extended to its present size a few years later in rubble masonry. Two arches in the east wall were blocked during the 1364–65 changes; the southern gave access to the former north aisle of the choir, the northern was an entrance to the earlier Chapel of St Godric. If you go out of the transept through the small doorway and look back, you can see the line of the steeply gabled roof of the chapel (rebuilt on the site of Godric's original wooden Chapel of St Mary) on the external face of the wall, and the line of its foundations is marked out on the ground. After the arches were blocked, two altars were set in front of them, the southern is thought to have been dedicated to St Cuthbert and the northern to St Godric.

Eastern arm

The choir of the church was divided from the rest of the church by a wooden screen, the sockets for which can still be seen in the eastern circular tower piers. Beyond were the choir stalls, their outline marked out on the turf. Here the monks would have sat for the services that made up the regular routine of the monastic day. On either side are three arcades, which, like those in the nave, were blocked up in 1364–65 when the present 'decorated'-style windows were inserted; one window on the north retains its reticulated ('net-like') tracery in relatively good condition. Some of the facing of the wall has been removed, probably during the nineteenth century, to expose the embedded pillars with their carved capitals.

Beyond the choir was the aisleless presbytery. The high altar, dedicated to St John the Baptist, stood against a wooden partition that divided off the far east end of the church. This space must have served as a sacristy where the holy vessels and other things used in the church ritual would have been

The south transept, showing the large window above the altar of St Mary

The whole of the interior of the church would have been plastered and painted in bright colours – the geometrical patterns on the choir piers, well-preserved when first laid bare, have now almost gone. This record was made in the 1920s

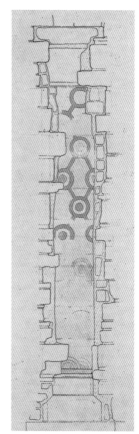

Double piscina

The north wall of the choir, showing the tracery windows inserted in 1364–65 when the arcades were blocked up

kept; the sockets for the screen can be seen in the side walls. On the south of the altar were four priests' seats or 'sedilia', recessed into the wall. Only the two western ones survive; the others, to the east, were destroyed when a large window was inserted in the fourteenth century. To the east of them, beyond the line of the screen, is a fine double piscina. The east end of the church, like the west end, originally had three tall lancet windows; it may have been deliberately demolished to create a view of the trees and river beyond, probably in the late eighteenth or early nineteenth century when the production of a 'vista' was very much in the public taste. The southern of the two tall octagonal pinnacles which flanked the original gable remains intact.

The Church of St John the Baptist

Both piscina and sedilia are set high above the floor, evidence that the floor level is now lower than it was in medieval times. This also accounts for the survival of the low walls of the eastern third of the earlier Church of St John the Baptist, which lay underneath the later medieval floor but are now exposed. This early church is that built by St Godric himself around 1150; it was excavated in the 1920s and a rough stone-built grave close to the north wall (its position now marked by a stone cross in the grass) is almost certainly that of

Godric himself. The foundations of the western part of the old church are simply marked out on the turf; those of the east end survive to a higher level because they were protected by the raised floor in front of the high altar. The church lies off-centre from its thirteenth-century successor, allowing a passage for the builders outside its north wall as the new building was raised around it before it was demolished.

CLOISTER

Now go back into the south transept and out through the door on the west into the cloister.

The north walk of the cloister is the best preserved – this was in fact the south aisle of the nave until the 1364–65 remodelling, when the original north walk was abandoned and the cloister enlarged. The traceried windows in the wall date from this period; originally the aisle wall would have been blank except for what are known as the east and west processional doorways – used during monastic ritual – at each end. Towards the east end of the wall a thirteenth-century wall-shaft survives from the original aisle, and would seem to indicate that it was intended to vault this part of the church. The eastern processional doorway now gives access to the east walk of the cloister, where only the bases of the broad windows that looked out on the central cloister garth survive. This walk was also rebuilt in the fourteenth century, as was that on the west, but the south walk retains the bases of the paired shafts which supported its original thirteenth-century arcade.

EAST RANGE

Walk along the east walk of the cloister.

Next to the church, with a central doorway flanked by a pair of windows, is the chapter house. Here the community would meet every day to hear a chapter of the rule, discuss priory affairs and consider matters of discipline. There are benches on the side walls and a low dais to the east, where the bench has a higher central seat, with stone arms, for the prior.

The remainder of the east range was remodelled in the later medieval period, and is a little difficult to understand. Next to the chapter house is a narrow passage, perhaps originally the inner parlour (where the monks would have been allowed some conversation) but later converted into a passage to the prior's hall. Beyond is a second parallel passage, where a short flight of wooden steps now provides the best access to the fifteenth-century kitchen, which was awkwardly sandwiched between the east range, reredorter on the south and prior's hall on the east. It still has its paved floor, with a massive fireplace on the east and a number of circular ovens.

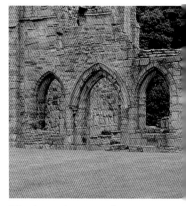

The chapter house seen from the south walk of the cloister

A section through the refectory, looking south, from Perry and Henman's mid-nineteenth-century survey

This is also the best place to view the reredorter – the monks' latrine block. A ledge or set-back marks the level of the wooden floor and seating. Underneath is a deep basement or pit, cut right down into the bedrock; the only exit is an arched opening at one end into a pit (now grilled over), from which it could be cleared. Reredorters were usually flushed by a stream running through, but the lie of the land here, and steep banks of the Wear further upstream, were not conducive to such engineering works. The manner in which the north wall of the reredorter partly blocks a window in the east range shows that it is a later addition.

The south end of the east range contains further later medieval sub-divisions, and a rounded projection in the north-east corner built out to accommodate one of the kitchen ovens. At first-floor level here – and over the whole of this range, including the chapter house – was the monks' dormitory; a ledge marks the level of its floor. Looking back at the gable of the south transept, the weathering of its low-pitched lead roof can still be traced.

The monks reached their dormitory by means of the night stair in the south transept and also, in the earlier years of the monastery, by a separate day stair set in the narrow gap between the east and south ranges. A doorway from this (now blocked) survives, high in the west wall near its south end; opposite is a doorway to the latrines in the reredorter.

SOUTH RANGE

The south range of the cloister, is formed by the monks' dining hall, or 'refectory', set above a half-sunken basement or 'undercroft'. It has been dated to c.1320 but may be a remodelling of a thirteenth-century building. It is built of large squared blocks of stone, in contrast to the rubble of the thirteenth-century structures to east and west. Two sets of stone steps lead down into the impressive undercroft, one (a later insertion) from the cloister walk and one from the open passage at the east end of the range. The undercroft has a ribbed vault supported by octagonal piers and alternating single and triple wall-shafts; the wall shafts have moulded capitals but the piers have none. On the south is a line of small square windows, some with vestiges of their old iron grilles. The rear arches of most have been crudely cut away, presumably to admit a little more light.

Return to the cloister and climb up the steps into the refectory.

Originally this room occupied the full length of the range, but was later subdivided to create an entrance lobby and a small room at the west end, with a larger room above. The refectory was lit by an impressive range of lancet windows on the south, shorter and broader than the earlier ones in the church. An upper storey was added at a later date; its square-headed windows can be seen high up above the lancets, with its floor supported on a row of central wooden pillars, now gone. The upper chamber at the west end has a

The west end of the refectory, showing the first-floor fireplace and window/chimney above. This peculiar piece of architectural ingenuity also occurs at the Prior of Durham's hunting lodge at Muggleswick

fireplace with its flue rising to an interesting window-cum-chimney in the gable (best seen by going outside the west wall of the cloister).

The impressive stone-vaulted undercroft to the refectory

The interior of the refectory looking east

Inside the building in the west range, showing the remains of its stone-vaulted lower floor

One would expect the refectory to be served by a kitchen outside its west end; there are some walls here, and what looks like a latrine pit, but these may be the result of later changes. Outside the guardianship area the footings of a square building just show through the turf. This may be the original kitchen but it has never been excavated.

WEST RANGE

It is unclear whether a full range of buildings was ever completed on the west side of the cloister, where one might expect to find store rooms, and probably a guest house.

There is one building, a small but high-status residential block, at the north end, however, which seems to have been constructed from one end of a larger, and possibly unfinished, structure. A tall tower-like building with a rib-vaulted basement, it is very complex structurally; access seems to have been by a short external flight of stairs outside its north wall, alongside the west door of the church. A small window that looked down into the south aisle of the church (later the north cloister walk) seems to be an original feature here, suggesting that its occupant may have had some responsibility for the church and its fittings.

THE PRIOR'S HOUSE

From the west range, go back into the church, past the tower crossing and turn right through a gap in the wall of the choir.

Facing you are the steps to the porch to the Prior's House, which occupies the whole of this area in what was once a walled enclosure on the south side of the eastern arm of the church. In plan it is very like a secular manor house of the period, and may have been consciously modelled on the Prior's Lodging in the parent monastery of Durham. It was extensively remodelled later in the medieval period, perhaps to accommodate the 'holidaying' monks.

The ground falls away eastward, and the range is built above basements or undercrofts, the vaults of which have largely collapsed, so there is today no access to the main rooms on the first floor. However, you can get a good view by going up the steps into the porch – the Account Rolls date this to 1464–65 – and looking through the main door into what was the prior's hall, heated by a fireplace on the north. Beyond, above the second section of under-croft, was the prior's 'camera', or personal apartment (the phrase 'in camera' is still used to imply privacy). Two further rooms opened from this – the chapel to the right and to the left what is thought to have been the prior's study, in a block of building that became known for some reason as the Douglas Tower.

The three sections of the under-croft of the range all have different types of vaults. All the vaults seem to have been inserted, re-using earlier responds in parts, probably taken from the demolished aisles of the church. Only the eastern section, which has a barrel vault, retains its vault intact.

The Douglas Tower is a four-teenth-century addition. The room at second-floor level had a fine oriel window on the north (its remains later known as the 'Wishing Chair') added in the fifteenth century. It is worth going back round the east end of the range to look at the prior's chapel (again on the upper floor); this had a gallery or loft at its west end, like the chapels of many secular manor houses. There was a further building on the south, little of which survives.

To the east and north of the Prior's House are the low remains of further buildings. Those to the east, towards the river, with a series of ovens, may have been a bakehouse and brewhouse. Those to the north, near the church, are more puzzling. Sir Charles Peers, who supervised the clearance of the ruins in the 1920s, interpreted these as a set of temporary monastic buildings erected c.1200, and in use while the church

and cloister were being built. Such buildings elsewhere are known from documentary evidence, but were almost always of wood. It is possible that parts of these buildings do date to this period, but there is so much evidence of change and modification

The prior's hall, and camera beyond, seen from inside the entrance porch

❖ THE WISHING CHAIR ❖

Most ruined abbeys and priories find a place in local folklore. At Finchale the remains of the oriel window at the north end of the Douglas Tower became known as the 'Wishing Chair'. The eighteenth-century antiquary Francis Grose reports that it 'was said to have the virtue of removing sterility and procuring issue for any woman who having performed certain ceremonies sat down therein'; he adds, rather cynically 'it may perhaps be needless to observe that since the removal of the monks it has entirely lost its efficacy'.

The Douglas Tower, showing the buttress that once supported the oriel window

that they would seem to have been in use over a long period of time (although parts were certainly disused by the time the Douglas Tower, which overrides their foundations, was built). The group may have served as the monastic infirmary; individual elements such as a hall, a kitchen and a latrine block (with a massive drain dropping towards the river) can be identified.

Return to the custodian's office by walking round the east end of the church.

It appears from the footings and plinths on the exterior of the east wall that the original plan included a full-length aisle to the sanctuary, but these were shortened as building proceeded. On the north side of the sanctuary are the remains of a building of uncertain use, with no direct access from the church. To the west of this the capital of one of the piers of the blocked arcade is exposed in the wall; its splendid high-relief carving of fruit and fir cones is well worth examining in detail.

THE PRECINCT

The precinct (walled enclosure) of
the priory was considerably larger
than the area now in guardianship.
Remains of several other structures
do exist, although these are not
accessible to the public. The
farmhouse, in line with the north
transept of the church, is a much-
altered medieval building and retains
a crown-post roof (a rarity in the
North of England), a fireplace and a
bay window overlooking the river. It
may have been the house of some
official attached to the community.

West of the priory would have
been an outer courtyard, containing
administrative and agricultural
buildings. The large barn here has
been much altered over the years,
but retains some medieval walling,
and seems to re-use roof trusses
from another building; the horse
engine house attached to it re-uses
thirteenth-century piers from the

*The spiral stair that led to
the wooden loft or gallery in
the prior's chapel*

nave. There are also the remains of
two gatehouses – the grassed-over
footings of the western and an ivy-
shrouded ruin of the southern – and
of parts of the precinct wall. Outside
the wall, to the south, were a series of
fish ponds.

*The priory ruins from the
west*

HISTORY

GODRIC AND HIS HERMITAGE

Mid-nineteenth-century lithograph of the view across the cloister, before the excavation and clearance of the remains early in the twentieth century

Finchale Priory has an unusual history but, as often with medieval monasteries, its beginnings and rise in importance are inextricably linked to one man, in this case St Godric. Godric, pirate-turned-saint, is a remarkably romantic figure whose long and varied life deserves to be better known.

Godric was born, probably in Norfolk, perhaps about the time of the Norman Conquest in 1066. As a boy he became a travelling pedlar, and when he was about twenty years old made the first of his journeys to Rome, a serious undertaking in the eleventh century. Travelling was in his blood, and he soon became a seaman; by about 1090 he was part-owner of a merchant ship and made voyages to Scotland, Denmark and Flanders. During his travels to Scotland he frequently visited Holy Island and also the Farne Islands, where stories of St Cuthbert's life as a hermit clearly left a deep impression on him. Later he took his ship to the Mediterranean, and it is probable that he was the 'Guderic, a pirate from the Kingdom of England' who is recorded as taking King Baldwin I of Jerusalem from

The similar view today

Arsuf to Jaffa. The term 'pirate' may not then have had its later connotations, and might mean no more than an independent merchant seaman. Godric was clearly still of a spiritual frame of mind, for soon after he made a pilgrimage to the shrine of St James at Compostela in north-west Spain; he then returned to England again, but before long he was off on his travels once more. These included two more pilgrimages to Rome, on the second of which, rather surprisingly, he took his mother with him.

When he was around forty Godric made a radical change in his lifestyle, abandoning seafaring to become a hermit. He first settled down in 1104 near Carlisle, then moved to live with another hermit at Wolsingham in Weardale. Here he had a vision of St Cuthbert in which he was told that he would find a new place to settle called 'Finchale', which at the time he had never heard of.

In 1106 his older companion died, and Godric set out on one last pilgrimage, this time to Jerusalem, before returning to the North East. After some time near Whitby, he came to Durham, where the community of Benedictine monks were able to inform him where his promised abode at Finchale lay. Ranulf Flambard, Bishop of Durham, gave him permission to settle there in 1112 or soon after. Godric seems to have first set up a hermitage about 1.6 km up river of the present priory, at a spot still known as Godric's Garth, where there are some slight ruins of old buildings that still await proper investigation. Subsequently he moved to the present site and built himself a hut with a turf roof, and a chapel in which he had a crucifix, an image of the Virgin Mary, and a bell. His life was not totally solitary, for his mother, brother and sister all came to live nearby.

Although the medieval chroniclers imply that the site was waste before Godric came, Roman pottery found during the 1920s suggests there may have been a villa or some other settlement nearby, and there are some suggestions that there may have been an earlier Christian site here.

In addition to the self-imposed hardships of wearing a hair shirt and chain mail, and sleeping with a stone as a pillow, Godric's life as a hermit was not easy. He was robbed and almost killed by marauding Scots, then narrowly survived a great flood in about 1150. In thanksgiving for this escape he built a new church, dedicated to St John the Baptist, which he linked to his earlier St Mary's Chapel by a thatched walk or cloister. His life of unremitting asceticism at last came to an end, after eight years bedridden and living on milk, on 21 May 1170; he is thought to have been 105, a remarkable age at this period. He was buried where he had lain in his last illness, against the north wall of St John's Church.

Reconstruction drawing by Peter Dunn of the hermitage as it may have appeared soon after Godric's death in 1170. The chapels of St John and St Mary are linked by Godric's thatched 'cloister'

❖ HERMITS AND SAINTS ❖

Godric of Finchale stands in a long tradition of solitary ascetics. Their lives were recorded by biographers, usually monks, and it is often difficult to disentangle fact and pious legends. Godric's biographer was Reginald, probably one of the two Durham monks who moved into his hermitage after his death. Although the visions of the saints and supernatural healings that Reginald describes are not accessible to modern enquiry, Godric's life and movements seem to be firmly rooted in history and are attested from a variety of sources. Some of his characteristics echo those of the Celtic saints, and in particular Cuthbert. Whether Godric consciously modelled himself on Durham's patron saint, or whether Reginald was keen to point out the parallels, is not clear. Both Cuthbert and Godric shared a liking for animals – Godric even tolerated snakes sharing his hut (he on one side of the fire and they on the other) – and both found prolonged immersion in cold water an aid in concentrating the mind on prayer, Cuthbert in the sea off Farne Island and Godric is a specially constructed 'great earthenware vessel' in the north-west corner of his chapel.

St Godric, in an illustration from a fourteenth-century manuscript of his hymns in English. The melodies to these hymns are also ascribed to Godric, which would make him the earliest known English composer

Reconstruction drawing by Peter Dunn of the priory in about 1320. Note the uncompleted west range

HENRY OF LE PUISET FOUNDS A PRIORY

After Godric's death, the Durham community sent two monks, Reginald and Henry, to occupy Godric's hermitage. In effect, Finchale became a cell, a small subordinate monastery, to the Cathedral Priory of Durham, but it received no more than a trickle of endowments for twenty-five years or so, until an interesting series of events took place. Henry of Le Puiset, son of Bishop Hugh of Le Puiset of Durham, wanted to found a new monastery, as so many major land-holders of the period did to ensure continued prayers for themselves and for their families. He turned to the Augustinian canons of Gisborough (in Cleveland, also in the care of English Heritage), perhaps because the resources required to establish a house of canons were less than those needed for a Benedictine monastery. Augustinian, or Black Canons (so called from the colour of their robes), also served as priests for parish churches, unlike the Benedictine monks of Durham, who rarely left the precincts of their monastery.

The canons from Gisborough settled first at Haswell, but finding the site too exposed, soon moved to Baxterford, in the Browney valley 2 km west of Durham. The Benedictine monks of Durham were unhappy at having a monastery of a rival order so close, and as soon as Henry's powerful father, Bishop Hugh, died in 1195 they brought pressure to bear on Henry, who was duly 'moved by penitence' as the chronicler records. In 1196 the Benedictines and Henry came to an arrangement: they would grant him Finchale, on condition that he promptly return it to them, along with the possessions he had previously granted to the Augustinians; in return he would be regarded as the founder of a new Benedictine priory at Finchale. It was a neat solution to a potentially troublesome problem. The Augustinians did not, however, give up without a fight and the Durham monks appealed to the Pope for the appointment of local adjudicators who then required that the title deeds to Baxterford's possessions should be surrendered.

Thus Finchale became a priory. Initially there appear to have been ten monks, but a grant made in 1278 specified that there should be five extra members, to assist in entertaining the pilgrims and poor who were flocking to Godric's grave. The old Church of St John the Baptist (in which the saint was buried) seems to have remained standing while a new church was built around it; Godric's older chapel, dedicated to St Mary, was rebuilt on its old foundations, and linked to the north transept of the new church. Building took several decades; it has been suggested that the construction of the main buildings was not embarked upon until the 1230s. Sir Charles Peers identified the remains of buildings east of the new church as those of temporary monastic buildings used during this period, but his interpretation remains somewhat uncertain. In 1239 the Bishop of Whithorn dedicated three altars, the high altar to St John the Baptist and two others to the Blessed Virgin and St Cuthbert; this may mean that at least the eastern arm of the church was complete.

THE 'HOLIDAY PLACE'

During the first half of the fourteenth century the size of the Durham community shrank considerably, largely as a result of the substantial loss of revenues brought about by damage inflicted during the recurrent warfare between the English and the Scots. Records suggest there may have been as few as five monks resident at Finchale, and that its buildings were in poor repair. The monks' response to this was two-fold: to reduce the size of the monastic church and buildings, and to emphasise an alternative role for the priory itself, that of holiday retreat for the monks of Durham. This function may have already begun in the later thirteenth century – Prior Hugh of Darlington spent at least some of his first retirement here – and continued until the Dissolution.

The surviving Account Rolls of the priory document many of the later changes to the buildings. Between 1364 and 1367 the church was reduced in size. It is recorded as being reconsecrated in 1367, the wording used may imply that the building needed to be cleansed after pollution by bloodshed – history unfortunately provides no further details. At the same time, the Prior's

Reconstruction drawing by Peter Dunn of the monastery on the eve of the Dissolution, c.1530. The church has been reduced in size, while an upper storey has been added to the refectory, the dormitory reroofed, and the Prior's House remodelled and expanded to accommodate the visiting monks

House was renovated, and this seems to have become the focus of this final phase of communal life. Some of this work seems to have been undertaken by John Lewyn, the most important provincial architect of medieval England. His career is well-documented; as well as the magnificent monastic kitchen at Durham he was responsible for work on the castles at Bolton, Dunstan-burgh, Roxburgh and Carlisle. The older buildings around the cloister seem to have been less used in the later medieval period, although in 1490–91 the dormitory was being re-roofed.

Statutes drawn up in 1408 spell out the rules under which the 'holiday place' operated. There were to be a prior and four monks permanently at Finchale, to be joined, every three weeks, by a further four monks from Durham. On alternate days two of the four holidaying monks were to attend the usual round of services, while the other two, having attended Mass and Vespers, had leave to walk 'religiously and honestly' in the fields. How strictly they followed these instruc-tions is not clear; there are references to Finchale monks being reprimanded for keeping sporting dogs, and attending hunting meets.

The position of prior of Finchale was one of the most highly prized offices open to Durham monks, and was often filled by men of academic distinction. Uthred of Boldon, four

times Prior of Finchale in the second half of the fourteenth century, was a theologian and spiritual writer of some repute, and was one of King Edward III's ambassadors to the Pope at Avignon. He died at Finchale in 1397, and was buried at the entrance to the choir. Other priors were remembered in a different way; the alacrity with which the last one, William Bennett, married when he considered that the Dissolution had released him from his monastic vows gave rise to a local proverb: 'The Prior of Finkela hath got a fair wife, and every monk will have one'.

DERELICTION AND DECAY

We know relatively little about the history of the buildings after the disso-lution of the priory in 1538. Some parts of the buildings remained in use, including perhaps the Douglas Tower, but most fell into ruin. In the eighteenth century, when ruins and romantic landscapes became popular, there may have been some selective demolition (perhaps the east end) to 'improve' the appearance of the site; alternatively, there may have been more practical motives, as when piers from the south nave arcade were re-used in a horse-engine house on the adjacent farm around 1800. In about 1830 the interior of the church was cleared, and the architectural details of the ruin were given some 'fostering

The doorway to the refectory

TOP RIGHT: *Decorated lead grille from the refectory that possibly formed a part of a larger ventilator (drawing by Chris Evans of original in Sunderland Museum)*

ABOVE: Lead ampulla, or small container for holy water, found at the priory. These were often sold to pilgrims at shrines

RIGHT: the reverse of a seal of Pope Honorius III (1210–27), found at the priory and once attached to a papal 'bull' or document. It shows the heads of St Paul and St Peter

(drawings by Chris Evans of originals in Sunderland Museum)

and judicious attention' by one of the Durham prebendaries. In 1836 the Surtees Society published the Account Rolls and much of the surviving documentation of the priory, providing historians with an invaluable tool towards their interpretation of the remains, and in the 1860s a fine series of measured drawings were made by Perry and Henman.

By the first decade of the twentieth century the ruins had been enclosed in an 'unclimbable iron fence' and the then owners, the Dean and Chapter of Durham, were charging visitors a one penny admission fee. Natural decay and vandalism continued however; and when the Architectural and Archaeological Society of Durham and Northumberland visited Finchale in 1914 Canon Brown noted that a large portion of the vaulting of the Douglas Tower had fallen and that there had also been 'some damage to the crypt [the refectory undercroft] as a result of horse-play by trippers'. Soon afterwards the Office of Works, the predecessor of English Heritage, came to an agreement with the owners and took the priory into guardianship.

GODRIC'S GRAVE REDISCOVERED

In the 1920s, Sir Charles Peers supervised the clearance of fallen debris from the ruins, and excavated some areas. He traced the foundations of

Godric's Church of St John the Baptist, inside the thirteenth-century eastern arm of the monastic church, and uncovered an empty stone coffin exactly where the chronicler describes the saint's grave as lying, against the north wall. The coffin was only 1.57 m long inside, tapering from 41 cm at the shoulders to 17 cm at the foot, its dimensions a vivid reminder of the slight stature of Godric, and his wasted frame after his last illness. The coffin seemed to have been lifted a little, so that its raised lid, of polished Frosterley 'marble' would

The priory from the north-east

be seen in the floor of the rebuilt church.

However, the coffin was found empty, and only one fragment remained of its smashed lid. Were Godric's mortal remains simply discarded by grave robbers at the Dissolution (when there is evidence of many graves in monastic churches being disturbed), or were they spirited away to safe keeping with some pious family? We may never know.

FURTHER READING

Peers, C.R. (1927) 'Finchale Priory' *Archaeologia Aeliana* IV (4th series) 193–220. A general historical account and description, with details of areas excavated in the 1920s.

Perry & Henman (1867) *Illustrations of the Medieval Antiquities of County Durham*. Includes 18 plates of Finchale with much large-scale drawing of architectural detail.

Roberts, E. (1867) 'On Finchale Priory, Durham' *Journal of the British Archaeological Association*, XXIII, 67–85. Mid-Victorian account with a drawing and plan.

Surtees Society (1837) Vol.2 *'The Priory of Finchale'*. Reprints most of the surviving documentation including the Account Rolls (in Latin).

Wilson, P.R. (1994) 'Finchale Priory, County Durham, Structural Analysis of "The Guest House"'. *Durham Archaeological Journal* 10, 55–60.

ACKNOWLEDGEMENTS

Thanks to Rodney Hawkins, and to Alan Piper of the University of Durham for the benefit of his knowledge of the medieval documentation referring to the life of St Godric and the later history of Finchale.

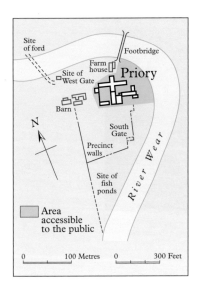

Site of ford
Footbridge
Farm house
Site of West Gate
Priory
Barn
South Gate
Precinct walls
Site of fish ponds
River Wear

N

Area accessible to the public

0   100 Metres   0   300 Feet

Late 12th century

Early 13th century

Various 13th century

14th century

Various 15th century

Post Suppression

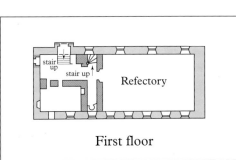

stair up
stair up

Refectory

First floor

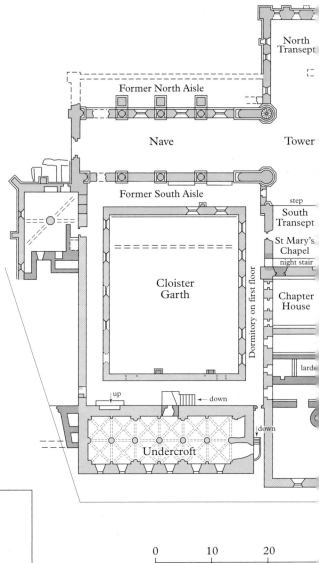

North Transept

Former North Aisle

Nave

Tower

Former South Aisle

step

South Transept

St Mary's Chapel

night stair

Cloister Garth

Dormitory on first floor

Chapter House

larde

up   down

Undercroft

down

0   10   20

0   50